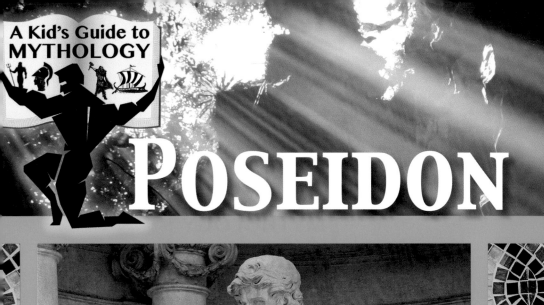

A Kid's Guide to
MYTHOLOGY

# POSEIDON

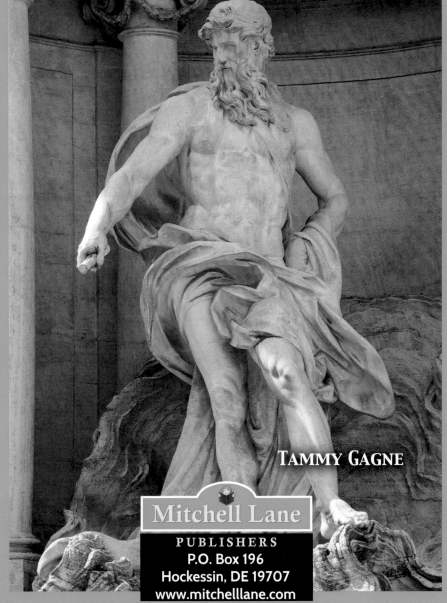

TAMMY GAGNE

Mitchell Lane
PUBLISHERS
P.O. Box 196
Hockessin, DE 19707
www.mitchelllane.com

**Mitchell Lane**

**PUBLISHERS**

Printing      1      2      3      4      5      6      7      8

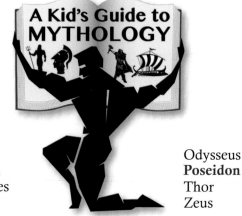

A Kid's Guide to
MYTHOLOGY

| | |
|---|---|
| Apollo | Odysseus |
| Athena | **Poseidon** |
| Hercules | Thor |
| Jason | Zeus |

Library of Congress Cataloging-in-Publication Data
Gagne, Tammy, author.
 Poseidon / by Tammy Gagne.
    pages cm. — (A kid's guide to mythology)
 Summary: "Many of the statues of Poseidon throughout the world are near the ocean since Poseidon is the god of the sea. The Greek gods and goddesses bring to mind images of heroes and heroines much admired by the Greek people. Poseidon fits this description to a certain degree, but like humans, he possesses many character flaws. Most of the stories about Poseidon depict an angry, vengeful being who makes decisions based on his emotions—he is a troublemaker for humans—and other gods and goddesses, and they in turn, are mischief makers for Poseidon. The myths are exciting, adventurous stories that the ancient Greeks used as guidance in their daily lives to explain nature and why things happened."
— Provided by publisher.
 Audience: Ages 8 to 11
 Audience: Grades 3 to 6
 Includes bibliographical references and index.
 ISBN 978-1-68020-012-6 (library bound)
 1.  Poseidon (Greek deity)—Juvenile literature. 2.  Gods, Greek—Legends—Juvenile literature. 3.  Mythology, Greek—Juvenile literature.  I. Title.
 BL820.N5G34 2015
 292.2'113—dc23
                                                                                                 2015017152

eBook ISBN: 978-1-68020-013-3

PUBLISHER'S NOTE: The Internet sites referenced herein were active as of the publication date. Due to the fleeting nature of some web sites, we cannot guarantee they will all be active when you are reading this book.

To reflect current usage, we have chosen to use the secular era designations BCE ("before the common era") and CE ("of the common era") instead of the traditional designations BC ("before Christ") and AD (anno Domini, "in the year of the Lord").

DISCLAIMER: Many versions of each myth exist today. The author is covering only one version of each story. Other versions may differ in details.

                                                                                                           PBP

# CONTENTS

Words in **bold** throughout can be found in the Glossary.

*Although he is a Greek god, Poseidon is known throughout the world. This statue of him stands outside the Hansa Venetian Hotel in Thailand.*

# 1

# THE GOD OF THE SEA

Your assignment for the weekend is to write a paper about Poseidon (po-SY-don)."

It was nearly the end of the school day on a Friday. The students were thinking about their plans for the weekend as buses lined up outside the school.

Ms. Platz brought the students back from their daydreams. "Can anyone tell me who Poseidon is?"

"He is god of the sea," Annie shouted proudly, sure that she had given the correct answer.

"No he's not!" argued Mason. "Neptune is the god of the sea. Isn't that so, Ms. Platz?" He was certain that he was right since he had been reading about Neptune.

Annie folded her arms across her chest and puffed out a breath of air. She was usually the first student to answer the teacher's questions, and she couldn't wait to see Mason proven wrong.

Ms. Platz looked at the two competitive students and smiled. "You're both right. In Greek mythology Poseidon is the god of the sea. But yes, in Roman mythology the god of the sea is Neptune. It looks like we will all learn a thing or two next week," she added just before the bell rang.

## The Reasons Behind the Myths

Greek mythology began as a way of explaining nature and why things happened. Why did the sun rise each morning and set each night? Who controlled the ocean and the tides? What made two people fall in love? In ancient Greece, humankind was still centuries away from fully understanding the science behind some of those occurrences. Even today we don't know all the answers. But in ancient times, myths provided exciting and magical answers for how the world came to be, and why everything happened the way it did. People all over the world are still drawn to Greek mythology, whether they take the stories **literally** or not.

As one journalist explained it, "Old myths die hard and some never do. . . . And they turn out to be popular far beyond where they originally flourished. The Greco-Roman **pantheon** can be a good example."[1] Those stories have inspired the creation of great paintings and sculptures, poetry and plays, and books and films. Greek mythology has even influenced the English language. The words atlas, echo, and **odyssey** all came from Greek myths.

## Even Gods Have Faults

The characters in Greek mythology are a big part of what makes the stories so interesting. Many people imagine gods as being so powerful that they couldn't possibly make mistakes. People hearing the myths for the first time also might not expect gods and goddesses to feel human emotions like jealousy or greed. But a great many of the stories are based on the faults of those larger-than-life characters and the poor choices they made.

Like Annie and Mason, Poseidon and Athena (a-THEEN-a) competed with each other. Each wanted to be the most loved **deity**. In one story both Poseidon and Athena (the goddess of wisdom) were determined to make the Greek people adore them. They decided to hold a contest—the winner would rule the Greek city by the sea where the challenge took place.

Poseidon created a massive storm to show humans how mighty he was, but his intentions were not all bad. He wanted to show the Greek people that he could protect them from terrible things like the weather and the raging waves of the ocean. Instead, he ended up frightening them. Athena used her intelligence to make Poseidon look bad. She easily won over the humans by offering them an olive tree, which could feed them and shield them from harmful storms.

Poseidon too offered the Greek people a gift—a saltwater spring. But they soon realized that the sea water he filled it with was undrinkable. Again, Athena came through as the clear winner. Known for his quick temper and for holding grudges, Poseidon was furious when the people decided to name the city Athens after the goddess. The story offers a great lesson about staying calm and using reason in important situations.

**Cry Me an Ocean**
According to one myth, it was actually Poseidon's strong emotions that led to the creation of the world's oceans. Poseidon and Zeus were brothers. But Zeus' wife Hera (HAIR-a) didn't always get along with the impulsive god of the sea. Hera began taunting Poseidon. She reminded

him that he wasn't nearly as powerful as his brother—his younger brother at that.

Poseidon responded to her hateful comments by throwing a temper tantrum. When people get mad, they may yell. But when gods get angry they cause earthquakes, hurricanes, and tornadoes. And so Poseidon's temper tantrums were destructive.

Hera didn't take Poseidon seriously, and she rolled her eyes at him, which made him angrier. After he released all his fury, he sat down on Mount Ida and wept. The salty tears that fell from his eyes flowed so forcefully that they formed the oceans throughout the world.

The *Republica* newspaper explains that Poseidon ruled over more than the seas. "He was also known as the 'Earth-shaker' because the myth is, he caused earthquakes. According to ancient Greek religion, in terms of power, Poseidon came second, just after Zeus . . . the supreme God himself. Poseidon was very powerful. He was usually portrayed carrying a **trident**, supposedly used to stir up storms."[2]

In Greece, about twenty kilometers (a little over twelve miles) from Athens, a temple still stands in honor of Poseidon. "Storms frequently resulted in shipwrecks and drowning," the *Republica* reported, "so mariners left gifts to make Poseidon happy at the temple at Cape Sounion. The original temple of Poseidon was built during the archaic period (800 BC—480 BC), out of tufa (a kind of limestone). This was destroyed in 480 BC by the Persian troops. The current temple was built in 440 BC, over the ruins of the previous one."[3]

The Temple of Poseidon is located at Cape Sounion— about an hour away from the city of Athens.

# LOVE AND DESTRUCTION

In addition to his quick temper and long-held grudges, Poseidon is well known for his love of the ladies. Like Zeus, he fathered numerous children with different mothers. His wife was the sea **nymph** Amphitrite (AM-fi-triyt). When he first saw her, Poseidon knew that he wanted to be with her. But it wasn't love at first sight for Amphitrite. She swam away as fast as she could. Poseidon wasn't going to let her get away, though. The sea god sent all the creatures in the water after her. One, a dolphin named Delphinus (DEL-fee-nus), caught her. Delphinus sang Poseidon's praises to Amphitrite. Delphinus was so persuasive in fact that Amphitrite agreed to marry Poseidon. He showed his thanks to Delphinus by placing him in the sky as a constellation.

Amphitrite wasn't the only nymph to catch Poseidon's eye. When Scylla (SKEE-lah) began to show an interest in Poseidon, his wife wasn't pleased, and Amphitrite also had a bad temper. Amphitrite turned Scylla into a six-headed sea monster. Scylla paired up with another nymph— one of Poseidon's daughters. Charybdis (KA-rib-deez) had tried to make her father's kingdom larger by flooding the land. But Zeus quickly became wise to Charybdis' plan and stopped her by turning her into a whirlpool.

*This sculpture was created during the latter part of the second century BCE. It shows Poseidon and his bride Amphitrite at their wedding. Although Poseidon fell deeply in love with Amphitrite, she wouldn't be the only female who caught his eye.*

Writer James McCusker explains, "To the distress of many sailors in the ancient world, Scylla and Charybdis eventually occupied the opposite sides of the Straits of Messina, the perilous waters that separate Sicily from mainland Italy. Sailing that close to the monster on one side and the whirlpool on the other, a navigator's options became as narrow as the passage itself. The hazards of that passage were so widely known that 'between Scylla and Charybdis' became a common expression for heightened danger with few or no options. Somehow, in the wonderful, mysterious ways of human language, sailing between Scylla and Charybdis eventually morphed into 'stuck between a rock and a hard place.' It's certainly easier to spell."[4]

*Some Greek myths include some horrible and distasteful acts. Artist Peter Paul Rubens captured one such deed in his painting of the god Cronus devouring one of his sons.*

# IN THE BEGINNING

If Poseidon's story had been a fairy tale, it would have begun something like this: Once upon a time, three Greek gods were born. They were named Poseidon, Hades (HAY-deez), and Zeus. The brothers had three sisters named Hestia (HEST-ee-uh), Demeter (de-MEE-ter), and Hera. Cronus (CROW-nuhs) swallowed all but one of Poseidon's siblings at birth. Remember, this is a Greek myth—some amazing (and disgusting) things are possible in mythology.

## Going Back to the Beginning

To better understand Cronus, it helps to know something about his own creation. As author Amy Friedman explained, "In the beginning there was nothing but **chaos** in the world, surrounded by unending water, and a god known as Oceanus ruled over all. The goddess Eurynome (yu-RIN-ah-mee) wanted to create order, and so she separated sea from sky from land, and soon three new gods ruled: Gaia (GUY-a), or Mother Earth, Uranus (you-RAIN-us), who ruled the heavens, and Tartarus (tar-TA-rus), who ruled the terrible region beneath the ground."[1]

Gaia and Uranus were Cronus' parents. Shortly after Cronus was born, his father locked him and his siblings deep in the Earth. Although his siblings feared Uranus, Cronus would not hide from him. Instead, he watched and waited for the opportunity to change the situation.

Gaia was saddened and angered by Uranus's actions. She didn't understand how a father could treat his own offspring so horribly. She decided to help her children fight Uranus. To do this, she gave them an extraordinary **sickle**. The shiny blade of the weapon was unbreakable. After suffering such terrible treatment at the hands of their father, Gaia's children also feared her. Instead of accepting her gift, they ran and hid from her. But Cronus was different. He knew that the sickle was the way out of his prison.

Cronus waited until his father was sleeping, and then Cronus struck Uranus with the blade. The attack did not kill Uranus, but it made him weak and powerless. Where did Cronus find the courage to defend himself and his siblings? And why was he different from them? No one knew the answer. But one thing was certain—he didn't learn anything from his father's actions.

"Gaia, Cronus' mother, could see into the future," writes Friedman, "and she understood that all things change. She tried to teach this to her children, but Cronus just **scoffed** at her."[2]

The same traits that made him fearless also made him arrogant. "I will rule forever," he assured his mother. "That is my wish, and so it shall be."[3]

Still, Gaia tried to warn him that he was acting foolish. "One day, one of your own children will take away your power," she said. "That is the way of the universe."[4]

*Cronus listened to Gaia when it came to the sickle. He chose to ignore her warnings about the future, however.*

Cronus listened carefully, just as he did when he was held prisoner, but instead of being a better father than his own had been, he made similar choices. "[H]e vowed he would never let a child of his defeat him. Each time his wife Rhea (REE-a) gave birth to a child, Cronus stole into the nursery, lifted the baby from its cradle and swallowed it whole.

"When Gaia realized what her son was doing, she despaired. She decided she must do something to save the world from such cruelty and vanity, and so when Rhea next gave birth, Gaia was there by her side. When no one was looking, Gaia lifted the baby out of the cradle and hid him beneath her robes. Then she replaced the baby with a stone she had wrapped in a blanket."[5]

When Cronus demanded that Gaia hand over his son, she passed him the swaddled rock. Distracted by his desire to protect himself, Cronus swallowed the swaddled stone and sent his mother away. He did not realize that she took his son, Zeus, with her. She brought the baby to Mount Ida in Crete, where she asked a nymph named Amalthea (a-MAL-thee-a) to raise him in secret. "Care for this boy as if he were your own," she ordered. "Protect him from Cronus. Though Cronus is his father, he must never find this boy."[6]

## It Runs in the Family

Zeus inherited courage and determination from his father, and Zeus used it to fulfill Gaia's prediction. As you can imagine, the experience of being swallowed by their father left Zeus' siblings feeling humiliated. From the time Zeus was born, he knew nothing of humiliation. Strong and determined to get his way, he eventually freed his brothers and sisters. Zeus' brave actions against Cronus had just begun. Over the next ten years the gods and goddesses continued to fight against Cronus and his brothers and sisters, the Titans. Zeus' generation of gods and goddesses were known as the Olympians.

"When the war ended, and the world was theirs," states Friedman. "Zeus crowned himself the supreme god of the universe. Then he divided the world among his brothers and sisters, giving each a place to rule. Hestia was made goddess of the home; Poseidon, god of the sea; Demeter was goddess of the harvest; Hera of marriage and childbirth. Hades became god of the underworld where once Tartarus had ruled."[7]

## The Good and the Bad

One version of the story states that three brothers drew straws to decide who would rule different parts of the universe. Hades had the worst luck. Since he drew the short

According to one Greek myth, Hades ended up god of the underworld by chance. When he and his siblings drew straws, Hades chose the shortest one. This result meant that he would rule the part of the universe none of the others wanted.

straw, he was named the god of the underworld. Hades was also a place where the Greek people believed humans went when they died. Rather than complain, Hades chose to make the most of his role. He was determined to gather as many subjects for his new kingdom as possible and so he rewarded any person on earth who caused the deaths of others.

As the ruler of the dead, Hades had no power over the living. He depended greatly on others to help him increase the size of his underworld kingdom. He rarely even left it himself. Still, people on earth feared him greatly. They worried that even saying his name could lead them to die sooner rather than later. Once people traveled to the underworld, Hades rarely let them return to earth.

While Poseidon carried a trident, Hades carried a two-pronged staff. Just like Poseidon Hades used his staff in destructive ways to cause earthquakes. Unlike his brother Poseidon, Hades was stern and unemotional; he could also be compassionate at times. "After the musician Orpheus played his lyre in the underworld, Hades agreed that his dead wife, the nymph Eurydice, could return with him to the world of the living."[8]

None of the gods were entirely good or bad. Each one had his gifts and shortcomings.

*Orpheus playing his lyre*

# WHAT IS IT LIKE
# TO BE POSEIDON?

Actor Danny Huston played Poseidon in the 2010 remake of *Clash of the Titans*. When asked about his experience making the film, he said, "It is fun! It's sort of childlike. When I was a kid, I remember the mechanical owl in the original. It's dress-up. You don't take it all that seriously, but then suddenly you're there and the sets are fantastic, and I had the privilege of working with Liam Neeson and Ralph Fiennes. And then, you're into it and it becomes very serious. At the end of your day's work, you're like, 'What was that about?' We really believed that we're three Gods, but what fun to play Gods. Those kinds of films are just very expensive. It's outrageous, the amount of money that's spent. Just to take a [peek] at that is fun, too."[9]

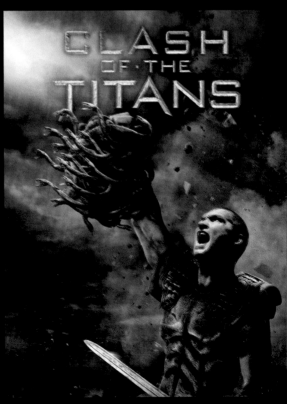

*Both the 1981 version of* Clash of the Titans *and the 2010 remake brought many of the Greek myths alive for the modern era. Each film introduced these ancient stories to a whole new generation of people.*

*Many people view Poseidon and the other Greek gods simply as characters from entertaining stories. To the ancient Greeks, though, Poseidon was a very real deity. Even some people today worship the sea god.*

# 3

# POSEIDON WAS REAL TO THE GREEKS

**M**any islands surround the mountainous **peninsula** of Greece. The ancient islanders, as well as the people living on the mainland, depended heavily on the oceans for their survival. The Ionian, the Aegean, and the Mediterranean Seas were filled with fish that fed the ancient people. The seas also served as routes to Egypt and other distant lands. Those sea routes created great opportunities for trade. It was an ideal situation—as long as the seas **cooperated**.

Strong winds and storms that churned the ocean waves made the everyday lives of fishermen and merchants dangerous business. Since they believed that Poseidon controlled the seas, the ancient Greeks began looking to him for good fortune. When wars erupted between the Greeks and their neighbors, navies fought their battles on the waters, and the people prayed to Poseidon to keep them safe.

## Art Imitating Life

Because Poseidon played such a meaningful role in the lives of the ancient Greeks, he can be found in numerous art forms from the period. Erin Averett is an Assistant Professor of Archaeology at Creighton University in

Omaha, Nebraska. She is also a **curator** for the Joslyn Art Museum, which featured an exhibit about Greek mythology in 2014. Averett considers Poseidon to be one of the three most influential Olympian gods, along with his brothers, Zeus and Hades.

"He's a very powerful deity," she states. "And because the sea is not always nice, Poseidon is not always a nice god. Even though he's one of the main ruling deities, you have to appease him. If you don't, your ship might get wrecked or be attacked by pirates or lost at sea. He's a god that could become angry very easily but he certainly has a lot of personality."[1]

Most people today think of Poseidon and his fellow gods as characters in entertaining stories. But to the ancient Greeks he was much more than entertainment. "The mythology section [of the exhibit] features objects that show Poseidon or a hero or divinity related to Poseidon, such as his son Theseus (THEE-see-us). The **cult** of Poseidon segment focuses on pieces that show the religious worship of Poseidon as well as items that may have been dedicated to him."[2]

Averett points out that the ancient Greeks faced many of the same challenges that people do today. "There are themes ancient Greeks dealt with about what it means to be human that we still struggle with today, especially things like worrying about natural disasters. The ancient Greeks just chose to deal with it by worshipping Poseidon and trying to make peace with him. Today we deal with it in different ways," she explained.[3]

Professor Averett was able to use the Poseidon exhibit as an educational project for her students. Each student researched a particular item that would be included in the show. The students were then asked to write summaries about what they had learned for the benefit of museum visitors. Averett used the best of those presentations in the final exhibit.

*Antoine-Louis Barye's sculpture of Poseidon's son, Theseus, slaying the Minotaur*

23

"The students were excited to do this," she said. "They had a wonderful time and they were chomping at the bit to see the show when it opened and hear the mobile stops they wrote. They are very invested in it and I think that's neat." A large marble statue of Poseidon and a fourteen-foot bronze trident were among the items on display. "I study objects like these all the time so I guess I am sort of **jaded** about it but these people were like, 'Wow, this object is 2,500 years old.' It amazed them that they were so close to these objects. And it was great to see them form connections to these people that lived in such a different culture so long ago."[4]

## A God of Land and Sea

Calamis, a sculptor who lived during the fifth century BCE created one of the most famous statues of Poseidon. The nearly seven-foot (1.2 meter) statue was **salvaged** from the sea off the coast of Greece in the early twentieth century. While the ancient Greeks worshipped Poseidon, the ancient Romans believed their god Neptune to be the ruler of the sea. Both gods were popular subjects for artists back then and in the centuries that followed.

"Since Calamis's day, there have been many sculptures of Poseidon and Neptune," explained Laurel Bowman. "The representations of the god invariably depict him as bearded and muscular and usually carrying his most famous attribute, the trident. Because of his association with water, statues of Poseidon are often found in fountains. Possibly the most famous of such statues is that found in the Trevi Fountain in Rome. It was created by Niccoló Salvi (1697–1751). It depicts the sea god in a chariot drawn by horses."[5]

Roman architect Niccoló Salvi designed the Trevi Fountain in Rome. Begun in 1732, the sculpture took many years to complete. When Salvi died in 1751, artist Guiseppe Panini took over the project, finishing it three decades after its start.

Some Greek myths also name Poseidon as the god of horses. He was even sometimes called Poseidon Hippon—the word *hippon* meaning "horse." The Roman poet Virgil claimed that Poseidon created the species by striking the earth with his powerful trident. Later he would help create a magical beast named Pegasus (PEG-uh-sus). As that story goes, the **Gorgon** monster Medusa (meh-DOO-sah) was pregnant with Poseidon's child when she was slayed by Perseus. As Perseus beheaded the snake-haired creature, a magnificent winged horse emerged from her neck.

Some ancient Greeks believed that one way to win Poseidon's favor was to **sacrifice** a horse in his honor. According to the Greek writer Pausanias, people in Argolis would lead the horses to the spring of Dine, "a spring of fresh water rising out of the sea."[6] They would then throw them into the water, where the animals would drown. Although this practice seems cruel today, sacrifices were a common practice in many ancient religions.

Journalist Jeffrey Weiss wrote, "These days, the ancient deities are the stuff of myth and legend. But three millennia back, people really believed in Zeus, Hera, and the rest of the Greek pantheon. This was religion, as unexceptional in its day as Baptists and Methodists are today. This old-time religion had plenty in common with modern faiths—and differed in some important ways . . . for instance, after an earthquake, people would pray and perform sacrifices in honor of the god of earthquakes. And they probably wouldn't have another earthquake for a while. Poseidon, not the **tectonic plates**, got the credit."[7]

# STILL GODS TO SOME

A small number of people still worship the Greek gods. In some countries, like the United States, people are free to practice whatever religions they choose. But in Greece, non-Christian religions are prohibited, with the exception of Islam and Judaism. As journalist Helena Smith shares, "For years, Orthodox clerics believed that they had defeated Greeks wishing to embrace the customs and beliefs of the ancient past."[8] But old belief systems are hard to change.

Vlassis Rassias thinks it is wrong for Christians to force their beliefs on others. "At school we were taught everything about the ancients except the way they worshipped. I found it very strange, and when I looked into it I began to see why. The Christians hated **pagans** so much that from the fourth century to the ninth century they destroyed their temples and libraries, killed their priests, closed their philosophical schools, and in one case, set up a death camp. It was genocide but priests don't want to talk about that today."[9]

Rassias and his fellow worshippers are calling for change from the Greek government. For one thing, they want to be allowed to conduct baptisms, weddings, and funerals with a view of the Acropolis on the Hill of Nymphs. "But our biggest demand is that our religion is accepted as a reality so that we can finally count just how many we are. If the intolerance continues we'll go to the European court of human rights."[10]

*Acropolis of Athens*

Homer was one of many Greek poets who told stories about the Greek gods and goddesses. He wrote the epic poems the Iliad and the Odyssey. Homer did not create the tales himself, but his celebrated verses helped pass the stories on to future generations.

# AN EPIC STORY

The ancient Greeks had an oral storytelling tradition and they had a collection of stories that explained the importance of each of the gods. "The Greeks had no universally accepted sacred text," points out Weiss. "They shared a series of tales handed down over centuries. The stories that Homer used in the *Iliad* and the *Odyssey* were particularly important. But other tales, some of which contradicted Homer and each other, were also important."[1]

Homer's epic poems serve as a significant source of what we know today about Greek mythology. While poems may seem short, Homer's works were anything but brief. The *Iliad* alone is more than fifteen thousand lines long and it is divided into twenty-four chapters. The *Odyssey* is also made up of twenty-four chapters, slightly shorter than the *Iliad*, and the *Odyssey* has twelve thousand lines.

## Tough Reads

The *Iliad* tells the story of the end of the Trojan War. And the *Odyssey* picks up where the *Iliad* leaves off. It tells the story of Odysseus (o-DISS-ee-us), who embarks on a difficult journey home to the island of Ithaca following the war. As writer Paul Roberts puts it, "Odysseus was looking forward to returning home to his faithful [wife] Penelope.

Instead he fell foul of the sea god Poseidon and was **buffeted** around the Mediterranean like a pea in a pinball machine. He did not reach his native Ithaca for ten years, after a series of hair-raising adventures involving storms, whirlpools, cannibals, **sirens**, vengeful gods, amorous goddesses, one-eyed giants, and six-headed monsters."[2]

As gruesome as it may seem, "the *Odyssey* teaches something more cheerful [than the *Iliad*]," states an *Irish Times* journalist, "that man, through his intelligence and adaptability, can sometimes overcome the [hatred] of gods and the [evil] of monsters. The particular god that the cunning and resourceful Odysseus . . . outsmarts in the course of his ten-year voyage home from Troy to Ithaca and his wife is the sea deity Poseidon, and the sea."[3]

Why is Poseidon so angry with Odysseus? Writer John Mullan explained, "In the *Odyssey*, the Cyclops [Polyphemus (pol-ee-FEE-mus)] is a one-eyed giant with a taste for human flesh. Polyphemus, a monstrous son of Poseidon, is the scariest of all. [Polyphemus] imprisons Odysseus and several of his men in his cave, killing and eating a couple of them each day. Odysseus manages to get him drunk and blind him with a red-hot stake."[4] Poseidon holds one of his famous grudges against Odysseus for this brutal—yet self-defensive—act.

No one knows exactly when Homer lived. But the best guesses place his lifetime around 750 to 700 BCE. Some historians claim that Homer was a blind **bard** who traveled from one place to another, telling his exciting tales. Others who study his work insist that Homer himself is a character—a combination of many different Greek bards who told those stories.

*Homer's tales of Odysseus became so popular that many artists created works depicting him. This one from about 660 BCE shows the warrior and his men blinding Polyphemus.*

Other poets, many unknown beyond their own lifetimes, wrote about the gods just prior to a large festival or other celebration. Those poems were used much like prayers are today. But because so many different people wrote them, each one was a bit different. The poems also varied greatly from one region to another. "Greece was not so much a nation as a set of city-states," explained Weiss. "Each had its own patron deity or deities. So worship in Athens was very different from worship in Sparta."[5]

## How Could They Believe That?

One might assume that the ancient Greeks were foolish to believe such far-fetched stories about gods and goddesses. But unlike many other religions, those ancient faiths did not demand that followers take the myths literally. The book *Greek Religion* states, "These tales were always taken with a grain of salt." Weiss agrees, "[The Greeks] didn't even demand that people completely believe them."[6]

Perhaps one of the reasons that many people did believe in the Greek gods was that no better explanation for the good and bad things that happen in everyday life existed at that time. "The era offered few material explanations for natural phenomena or human behavior: Illnesses, earthquakes, changing tides of war, bad people getting rich and good people suffering. . . . All seemed to defy logic. One way to make sense of a fractured world was to believe in a variety of squabbling powers," suggested Weiss.[7]

Because many of the gods were flawed, they were also viewed quite differently than modern deities. "The gods and goddesses were all too human," Weiss said. "As such, they were frequently the butts of jokes or ridicule."

Although Sparta wasn't far from Athens, the people in the former city-state worshipped differently. A figure called Lycurgus created the laws of this region. Like the people of Athens, though, he was said to seek guidance from the Greek gods.

Modern religions would definitely frown upon their followers making fun of their idols.[8]

Greek myths about Poseidon show both his best and worst qualities. "When he was in a good mood," stated Weiss, "the seas were calm and the winds favorable. On his bad days, he caused earthquakes and storms."[9]

Poseidon's temper often led him to revenge. That was the case after Odysseus blinded Poseidon's son, Polyphemus, in the *Odyssey*. Poseidon made it as difficult as possible for Odysseus to return home following the Trojan War. The angry god staged storm after storm to push Odysseus farther and farther from his island of Ithaca, nearly drowning him in the process.

But, before Poseidon could win that battle, Athena appeared, and when Poseidon wasn't watching, she helped Odysseus many times. Athena calmed the waters and guided Odysseus in the final stretch of his incredible journey, and she ruined Poseidon's plan. Poseidon's temper accomplished nothing.

*Athena statue in the Academy of Athens, Greece*

# STAR GAZING

If you are an astronomy fan, you may already know that many constellations have been given the names of Greek gods and other mythological creatures. But did you know that some people believe that Homer's poem the *Iliad* was actually meant to be a guidebook to the stars? Florence and Kenneth Wood wrote a book called *Homer's Secret Iliad*, which suggests just that.

Book reviewer Christian Tyler explained, "Born on a farm on the Kansas prairie, where the stars shine bright, Edna Johnston (Florence's mother) went on to be a teacher in England. She puzzled for years over the oddities of Homer's epic. Gradually she became convinced that the *Iliad* is a memory-aid for the movement of stars, constellations, and planets visible from the ancient Aegean. It was the coded knowledge of a pre-literate age, vital for land travel, nautical navigation, and agriculture."[10] No one knows for certain whether Johnston's theory is in fact the truth behind one of the most popular poems ever written.

*We may never know if Homer created his epic poem the* Iliad *to help people keep track of the moving constellations in the night sky.*

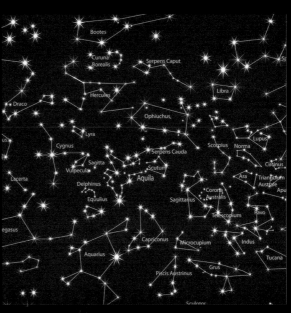

*Mount Olympus is not just a setting for Greek myths. It is also an actual mountain—the highest in the entire country of Greece. The mountain's highest peak, Mytikas, measures 9,573 feet (2,918 m) tall.*

# 5
# GOOD TO BE A GOD

The lives of the gods were anything but ordinary. Even their home was said to be remarkable. The Greek people believed that most of the gods and goddesses lived in a palace in the clouds over Greece's largest mountain. High above Mount Olympus, the surroundings were nothing short of paradise. Even the weather there was perfect.

That lofty site made it possible for the gods to watch everything happening below them on earth whenever they liked. Even though humans were never allowed to see or visit the home of the gods, the Greek people believed the gods were looking out for their best interests. When the gods strongly disapproved of what the humans were doing, some of them left their special home and traveled down to earth. It wasn't at all unusual for the Greek gods to interfere with events on earth, or even punish humans for their poor decisions. At least that is what the myths state.

Some gods also made the trip to earth for more selfish reasons. Despite being married to Hera, Zeus fell in love with several humans. He often traveled to earth to spend time with the latest woman who had recently caught his eye.

## Trouble in Paradise

Poseidon did not spend much time with the other gods above Mount Olympus since he had built his own underwater palace deep in the ocean. At first he hoped to share his palace with a water nymph named Thetis (THEE-tis). He pursued her with great passion in the beginning, but his greed cost him that relationship like so many others. When he learned that they would have a son who would grow to become more powerful than he was, Poseidon ended the relationship at once. The sea god eventually settled down. But like his brother Zeus, he wasn't faithful to his wife.

Many stories about Poseidon involved his bad decisions and the results from his bad actions. In one myth he conspired with Hera and Apollo (uh-POL-oh) to "bind Zeus in chains and suspend him in the heavens." The trio thought that Zeus had been acting too harshly. To fix the problem, they decided to take matters into their own hands, but the plan failed because of Thetis. The water nymph caught wind of their idea and told Zeus about the plot—perhaps because she held a grudge against her former lover Poseidon.

Zeus punished Hera for her part in the conspiracy by holding her by her heels over Mount Olympus. Even though that was a frightening consequence, Apollo and Poseidon faced a longer, harsher sentence. Zeus sent them to serve King Laomedon for an entire year. While they worked for him, they helped build the walls of the city of Troy. The king refused to pay the gods for their labors. Poseidon wasn't about to ignore that horrible insult, and he responded by sending a sea monster to destroy the king's land.

*Greek mythology is a mix of human nature and seemingly impossible events—such as Thetis turning into a lioness when attacked by Peleus.*

## A Brother-Sister Thing

In the original myths, Poseidon's shortcomings had much to do with sibling rivalry. Poseidon spent a great deal of time feeling envious of Zeus, who ruled the kingdom of heaven. But only one of them could take that important job. Although Poseidon accepted his role as god of the sea, a fair amount of arguing took place between the two brothers.

"The mythology of the Greek gods was very human," said history professor Gregory Elder. "They had loves and

*Poseidon and Zeus are just two of the major Greek deities. Among the others are Hera and Apollo—depicted here by artist Albert Henry Payne.*

hates, banquets, feuds and rivalries, just like their human creators. One can feel the . . . anger of Poseidon when Odysseus blinds his son Polyphemus."[1]

The original myths about Poseidon and the other gods were immensely popular with ancient audiences. "The Greeks . . ." Elder said, "were [quite open] about their religion, which made it by necessity more human and accessible to ordinary, uneducated people. Sacrifices were outdoors and mobs came to watch them. . . . Even the mythology was available more commonly. The ability to read and write was a status symbol, and education for the young, often males, was encouraged. Plato called Homer the 'educator of all Greece' and so his mythology was well known and publicly recited and even acted out on stages, so it had great popular appeal."[2]

# A Dramatic Temper Indeed

Poseidon's biggest flaw, his temper, gave Greek mythology some of its most sensational creatures. "Poseidon was responsible for most of the monsters who dwelled in the already dangerous waters of the sea," stated Laurel Bowman. "He could easily be offended and was capable of inflicting terrible punishments on mortals who slighted him. For example, Cassiopeia (KAS-ee-oh-pee-ah), queen of Ethiopia, once boasted that she was more beautiful than any of the Nereid's (NER-ee-idz), the sea nymphs who were the daughters of another sea god, Nereus (NER-ee-us). The Nereid's were so offended that they asked Poseidon to punish Cassiopeia. First, Poseidon sent a tidal wave that flooded her land. Then he sent a sea monster to attack her people."[3] Cassiopeia tried everything to get him to stop—including sacrificing her own daughter, Andromeda (an-DROM-uh-duh), to a sea monster. Luckily for Andromeda, though, Perseus rescued her at the last minute.

*Perseus fighting the sea monster to free Andromeda*

# CHAPTER NOTES

## Chapter 1: The God of the Sea

1. Vikas Datta, "Greek Gods in modern fiction," *Kasmir Monitor*, May 6, 2014, http://www.kashmirmonitor.in/news-greek-gods-in-modern-fiction-66359.aspx

2. ------, "Greece of myths and legends Cape of Sounion!" *Republica*, September 23, 2013, ProQuest.

3. Ibid.

4. James McCusker, "Olympia can't duck difficult decisions," *The Herald*, November 14, 2010, ProQuest.

## Chapter 2: In the Beginning

1. Amy Friedman, "The Children of Cronus A Greek Take," *South Florida Sun-Sentinel*, August 16, 2005, http://articles.sun-sentinel.com/2005-08-16/lifestyle/0508150052_1_cronus-gaia-zeus

2. Ibid.

3. Ibid.

4. Ibid.

5. Ibid.

6. Ibid.

7. Ibid.

8. Laurel Bowman, et al., *Gods and Goddesses of Greece and Rome*, Tarrytown, NY: Marshall Cavendish, 2012, 111.

9. Christina Radish. "Danny Huston Talks New Starz Series Magic City and Playing Poseidon in Wrath of the Titans," *Collider.com*, http://collider.com/danny-huston-magic-city-interview/

## Chapter 3: Poseidon Was Real to the Greeks

1. Cheril Lee, "Poseidon and the Sea: You know about the trident, now get the rest of the story," *The Reader*, February 14, 2014, http://www.thereader.com/comments/poseidon_and_the_sea/

2. Ibid.

3. Ibid.

4. Ibid.

5. Laurel Bowman, et al., *Gods and Goddesses of Greece and Rome*, Tarrytown, NY: Marshall Cavendish, 2012, 247.

6. Pausanias. *Pausanias' Description of Greece*. Amazon Digital Services, 2014, 381.

7. Jeffrey Weiss, "Gods behind the Games," *Amarillo Globe News*, August 21 2004, http://amarillo.com/stories/2004/08/21/fai_godgames.shtml

8. Helena Smith, "By Zeus!" *The Guardian*, January 31, 2007, http://www.theguardian.com/world/2007/feb/01/religion.uk

9. Ibid.

10. Ibid.

# CHAPTER NOTES

**Chapter 4: An Epic Story**

1. Jeffrey Weiss, "Gods behind the Games," *Amarillo Globe News*, August 21 2004, http://amarillo.com/stories/2004/08/21/fai_ godgames.shtml

2. Paul Roberts, "Relive the adventures of distant days: Noble Caledonia Mediterranean Follow in the footsteps of the ancient Greek hero Odysseus and discover a wealth of history on a fascinating Mediterranean odyssey, says Paul Roberts," *The Daily Telegraph*, April 30, 2014, ProQuest.

3. ------, "The Europeans, no 24: Homer: His origins, even existence, are in doubt, but the works attributed to him are fundamental to our culture," *Irish Times*, June 12, 2013, ProQuest.

4. John Mullan, "Ten of the Best Monsters in Literature," *The Guardian*, February 20, 2010, http://www.theguardian.com/ books/2010/feb/20/ten-best-monsters-in-literature

5. Jeffrey Weiss, "Gods behind the Games," *Amarillo Globe News*, August 21 2004, http://amarillo.com/stories/2004/08/21/fai_ godgames.shtml

6. Ibid.
7. Ibid.
8. Ibid.
9. Ibid.

10. Christian Tyler, "Homer's secret history of the night: The Iliad is actually a stellar guidebook, a poetic encryption of ancient astronomy and geography, according to a new book that maintains the 'wine-dark sea' refers not to the ocean, but to the sky," *National Post*, June 26, 1999, ProQuest.

**Chapter 5: Good To Be a God**

1. Gregory Elder, "Greeks had more relatable—and human— deities," *Redlands Daily Facts*, November 1, 2007, http://www. redlandsdailyfacts.com/general-news/20071101/greeks-had-more- relatable-and-human-deities

2. Ibid.

3. Bowman, Laurel et al., *Gods and Goddesses of Greece and Rome*. Tarrytown, NY: Marshall Cavendish, 2012, 244.

# WORKS CONSULTED

Bowman, Laurel et al., *Gods and Goddesses of Greece and Rome.* Tarrytown, NY: Marshall Cavendish, 2012.

Datta, Vikas. "Greek Gods in modern fiction." *Kasmir Monitor,* May 6, 2014. http://www.kashmirmonitor.in/news-greek-gods-in-modern-fiction-66359.aspx

Elder, Gregory. "Greeks had more relatable—and human—deities." *Redlands Daily Facts,* November 1, 2007.

Friedman, Amy. "The Children of Cronus A Greek Tale." *South Florida Sun-Sentinel,* August 16, 2005.

------, "Greece of myths and legends Cape of Sounion!" *Republica,* September 23, 2013.

Lee, Cheril. "Poseidon and the Sea: You know about the trident, now get the rest of the story." *The Reader,* February 14, 2014. http://www.thereader.com/comments/poseidon_and_the_sea.

Lui, John. "Immortal combats: Movie-makers love taking liberties with ancient deities and Immortals is the latest film to do that." *The Straits Times,* November 16, 2011.

McCusker, James. "Olympia can't duck difficult decisions." *The Herald,* November 14, 2010.

Mullan, John. "Saturday Review: Ten of the Best Monsters in Literature." *The Guardian,* February 20, 2010. http://www.theguardian.com/books/2010/feb/20/ten-best-monsters-in-literature.

Mutén, Burleigh. *Goddesses: A World of Myths and Magic.* Cambridge, Massachusetts: Barefoot Books, 1997.

Napoli, Donna Jo. *Treasury of Greek Mythology.* Washington, DC: National Geographic, 2011.

Ogden, Daniel. *A Companion to Greek Religion.* Hoboken, New Jersey: John Wiley & Sons, 2010.

Pausanias. *Pausanias' Description of Greece.* Amazon Digital Services, 2014, 381.

Philip, Neil. *The Illustrated Book of Myths.* New York: DK Publishing, 1995.

Radish, Christina. "Danny Huston Talks New Starz Series Magic City and Playing Poseidon in Wrath of the Titans." *Collider.com.* http://collider.com/danny-huston-magic-city-interview.

# WORKS CONSULTED

Roberts, Paul. "Relive the adventures of distant days: Noble Caledonia Mediterranean Follow in the footsteps of the ancient Greek hero Odysseus and discover a wealth of history on a fascinating Mediterranean odyssey, says Paul Roberts." *The Daily Telegraph*, April 30, 2014.

Smith, Helena. "By Zeus!" *The Guardian*, January 31, 2007. http://www.theguardian.com/world/2007/feb/01/religion.uk.

------, "The Europeans, no 24: Homer: His origins, even existence, are in doubt, but the works attributed to him are fundamental to our culture." *Irish Times*, June 12, 2013.

Tyler, Christian. "Homer's secret history of the night: The Iliad is actually a stellar guidebook, a poetic encryption of ancient astronomy and geography, according to a new book that maintains the 'wine-dark sea' refers not to the ocean, but to the sky." *National Post*, June 26, 1999.

Weiss, Jeffrey "Gods behind the Games." *Amarillo Globe News*, August 21 2004. http://amarillo.com/stories/2004/08/21/fai_godgames.shtml.

# FURTHER READING

Bryant, Megan E. *Mythlopedia: Oh My Gods*. Danbury, Connecticut: Franklin Watts, 2009.

Clayton, Sally Pomme. *Greek Myths: Stories of Sun, Stone and Sea*. London: Frances Lincoln Children's Books, 2012.

Rylant, Cynthia. *The Beautiful Stories of Life: Six Greek Myths Retold*. San Diego: Harcourt Children's Books, 2009.

Temple, Teri. *Poseidon: God of Sea and Earthquakes*. Mankato, Minnesota: The Child's World, 2013.

Townsend, Michael. *Amazing Greek Myths of Wonder and Blunders*. New York: Puffin, 2014.

# GLOSSARY

**bard** (BAHRD)—a person in ancient societies skilled at composing and singing or reciting verses about heroes and their deeds

**buffet** (BUF-it)—to pound repeatedly; also a cabinet for holding china and linen; also a meal laid out so that guests may serve themselves

**chaos** (KEY-os)—complete confusion

**cooperate** (koh-OP-uh-reyt)—to work with others for a common goal

**cult** (KULT)—a system of religious worship

**curator** (kyoo-RAY-ter)—a person in charge of a museum

**deity** (DEE-i-tee)—a god or goddess

**Gorgon** (GAWR-guhn)—one of three sisters in Greek mythology having snake-entwined hair and glaring eyes; people who looked at them turned to stone

**jaded** (JEY-did)—to become weary from having or seeing too much of something

**literally** (LIT-er-uh-lee)—understanding something according to the strict meaning of the words

**nymph** (NIMF)—one of many goddesses in old legends represented as beautiful young girls living in mountains, forests, meadows, and waters

**odyssey** (OD-uh-see)—a long wandering or series of travels

**pagan** (PEY-gun)—relating to religious beliefs other than those of the main world religions

**pantheon** (PAN-thee-on)—the gods of a particular mythology considered collectively, or a temple dedicated to all the gods

**peninsula** (puh-NIN-suh-luh)—a piece of land nearly surrounded by water or sticking out into the water

**sacrifice** (SAK-re-fiys)—the act of offering something precious to a god or goddess, especially the life of a person or animal

**salvage** (SAL-vij)—to save or recover from destruction

**scoff** (SKAWF)—to express with scorn or mockery

**sickle** (SIK-uhl)—a tool with a sharp curved metal blade and a short handle

**siren** (SIY-ren)—a tempting woman

**tectonic plates** (tek-TON-ik PLEYTZ)—geological structures that cause folding and faulting of the earth's surface; when they move they cause earthquakes

**trident** (TRYD-nt)—a spear with three prongs

# INDEX

# ABOUT THE
# AUTHOR

Tammy Gagne is the author of more than one hundred books for adults and children, including *Apollo* and *Athena* for Mitchell Lane Publishers. She resides in northern New England with her husband and son. One of her favorite pastimes is visiting schools to speak to children about the writing process.